Your guide to easy training

BUDGERIGARS

Paula Jones
Philippa Bower

Contents

Rainbow sits proudly on his favourite perch — a spray of artificial blossoms from where he can see out of the window. This is where he likes to practise his phrases.

Introduction

Our budgerigar, Rainbow, is a happy, healthy, loving pet who lives freely in our living room. He is caged only at night, although he often chooses to be in his cage during the day. He is friendly with visitors and enchants us all with his playful antics and his talking.

Rainbow comes to my hand on command, and speaks more than 20 phrases clearly and fluently. Because he has plenty of exercise and can fly freely around the room he is not prone to any of the health problems that can beset caged birds. He is also happy and has no desire to escape. Even though the door to our living room is often open, he rarely leaves the room which is his territory.

Many people have asked me how I have trained Rainbow. Although there are plenty of books on keeping budgies, few deal in depth with how to train a bird and I have found some new ways that you might like to try. For example, I have read that you should teach a phrase a word at a time. This is not the way I teach Rainbow: I use the entire phrase and, although he often picks out single words to practise, the whole phrase becomes set in his mind. If the phrase is very long I teach it in two halves which I then put together so Rainbow learns the phrase as a whole.

I have also read that a budgie should be left alone for a day or two after being purchased to give it a chance to 'settle down' in its new home. In my experience the first days are critical in establishing a relationship that will take the place of a budgie's bond with its parents. This means that you should be with your new budgie as much as possible.

I have written this book for the many people who have admired Rainbow and for all who want to get the most pleasure out of their budgie. Unfortunately, it might arrive too late for the many budgies who are too old to train and are spending their days confined to their cages. Some can be tamed with much effort and patience, but others are aggressive when approached and probably are impossible to tame.

For those who have failed in the past to train a budgie and feel regretful that their pet has not turned into the loving, happy companion they had hoped for, my advice is to find somebody who owns an aviary and ask if they would be willing to take your budgie. It is much kinder to let your bird join a flock and have room to fly than to keep it confined to a cage with too little exercise and companionship. Most aviary owners will be helpful and sympathetic and will probably let you come and visit your bird so you can see it is happy.

Once you have ensured that your old budgie has a happy home, do not feel reluctant to try again with a baby bird. As long as you are determined, and willing to show patience and perseverance then your bird could become an enjoyable companion. This book will show you how to achieve this pleasure. With the right attitude everyone can enjoy the company of these delightful, cheery, easy-to-look after pets. 'Do not give up' is perhaps the best advice this book can give.

Getting started

The first thing to do after deciding to buy a budgerigar is to buy the cage.

There are many excellent cages on the market. Buy a reasonably large one, but there is no need to waste money buying an enormous one; if you manage to train your budgerigar properly, he will be in it only at night. It can never be good for your budgerigar to keep him shut up in a cage all the time, however large it is. He will only be able to take the amount of flying exercise he needs by living freely in the room. However, if you cannot train your budgie, but want to keep him, then do buy a large, rectangular cage in which he can move freely. For the same reason, if your budgie is out of his cage most of the time, it does not really matter whether

the cage is round or square. Buy one that looks attractive in your living room. For example, we chose a pretty, round, pink cage that gives Rainbow plenty of room to hop around.

Although size and shape are not too important there are other aspects of the cage that are vital. You must choose a cage in which the door is sufficiently tall and wide for you to lift your new budgie in and out on your hand without hitting his head. The budgie will be nervous of being handled and it is very important to move your hand smoothly and slowly once you have persuaded him to perch on it. If you have to jerk and twist your hand to get it through the door he will be frightened and his worst fears will be confirmed if you knock him against the bars! Taking your budgie in and out of the cage is tricky even with a large cage door and virtually impossible if the cage door is too small or too narrow.

Different cages are designed for different birds. Ask the shop assistant to make sure you buy a budgie cage rather than one designed for a cockatiel or canary.

When you buy a cage it will have two built-in containers. Many people assume that one is for food and the other is for water. I find that it is much more convenient to use both of them for food and to buy a tubular water container that clips to the bars of the cage.

The reason for having two food containers is because the food becomes covered in hulls. When budgerigars eat, they nibble the outer layers (hulls) off the seeds to find the kernels. The hulls are left on the surface and it becomes an effort for the budgie to search through them to continue feeding. I put a couple of dessert spoonfuls of seeds into each container so that, when one of his food containers has too many hulls, Rainbow goes to the other one. Having said that, I recommend that for the first couple of weeks you fill the food containers right to the brim so your new budgie can find them easily. The containers should be emptied and filled with fresh seeds every 24 hours. A good tip is to transfer your seeds from their bag to a jug or jar with a lid, which keeps them fresh.

It is important that the seeds do not become contaminated by droppings, so choose a cage that provides appropriate protection for the seeds within the container. Rainbow's containers are on the outside of the cage and he feeds by putting his head through an opening in the bars.

A tubular water container protects the water from contamination. Change the water every 24 hours and wash the container. I have two water containers so that when I replace one, I can just put it by the sink and wash it at my leisure. Usually I use ordinary washing-up liquid and an old toothbrush reserved specially for the container.

When you give your budgie treats, such as spray millet or fruit sticks, attach them to the bars of the cage within easy reach. Rainbow also likes to nibble a piece of apple which I push between the bars. Remember that whatever food and water you place within the cage must be well away from the bird's droppings. Personally I prefer to feed Rainbow millet by hand. It is such a pleasure to watch his enjoyment. That way, too, I can control the amount he eats; too much of a rich food like millet would make him fat.

Even a new cage needs to be washed when you bring it home as it will have got dusty in the shop. A second-hand cage should be scrubbed, disinfected and thoroughly dried. Put a sheet of sandpaper on the floor of the cage, cutting it to shape if you have not been able to buy the exact size. The sandpaper should be taken out of the cage daily and any droppings brushed away. Budgie droppings are small, dry and easily removed. The sheet will need replacing once or twice a week.

Finally, clip a cuttlefish bone to the inside of the cage to provide your budgie with calcium (the mineral needed for strong claws, beak and feathers). Cuttlefish bones can be found on the beach sometimes but wash them well before you use them.

It is tempting to buy lots of toys and treats at this stage but do not give them to your

To recap
Choosing a cage for your free-flying budgie:
- Colour and shape do not matter
- The door must be wide and tall enough
- There should be two food containers

- Food and water containers should be protected from droppings

Preparing a cage:
- Wash the cage
- Line base of the cage with sandpaper
- Fill food and water containers
- Provide a cuttlefish bone

budgie straight away. His new environment will be frightening for him and it should be kept as simple as possible. Wait until at least the second day and then put a small toy (such as a mirror or ball with a mirror attached) at the bottom of his cage. It may take him a long time to approach it but at least he will get used to its presence.

The final position for your budgerigar's cage should be high in a corner of the living-room away from direct sunlight. Budgerigars are used to perching high in trees and looking down on their surroundings. However, during the first few weeks, have the cage on a bureau or bookshelf so that it is at eye level and within easy reach.

It is important to keep the bird away from bright light, including sunlight, spotlights

and strong internal lighting. It should also be as far away as possible from the television.

It is possible to buy a cage stand that will hold the bird at the correct level, but these tend to be easily knocked over. A stand will be needed only until your bird is tame so it may not be worth the investment. You need to have the cage at eye level to make it as easy as possible for you to lift the budgie in and out.

At this stage, even opening the cage door must be done with care, as a sharp click will frighten your new bird. Avoid any sudden sounds and movements during the first few days.

Dogs, cats and very young children should be kept out of the room until the bird is more confident. Older children can be allowed in but must move slowly and be very quiet. Gentle background music will create a soothing atmosphere and help to reduce the effect of unexpected noises. In time, a budgie will grow to love company, but it will always be frightened by sudden loud noises, and these should be avoided whenever possible.

Any inconvenience at the beginning is well worth while as a tame budgie is a fearless companion for children. It should also get on well with other pets. Beware of cats, however; the fluttering of feathery wings could cause even the gentlest to be overwhelmed by the hunting instinct. Some cats are inclined to be mousers and do not show much desire for birds. Only you know your cat well enough to decide whether to take the risk.

In the early days Rainbow was wary of the colour black, especially on strangers. He would never fly to visitors who were wearing black and sometimes was reluctant to come even to me when I was wearing that colour. So my final piece of advice before you set off to purchase your new bird is to change out of your black clothes into something bright and colourful to make your first approach as easy as possible.

To recap

Getting ready for the budgerigar:
- Put the cage at eye level, away from bright light
- Ban pets and young children from the room
- Do not wear black

How to choose your bird

Look for a male budgerigar as young as possible if you want a bird that will be easy to train and able to talk fluently.

The best place to start looking for your baby budgie is in a large pet centre with a rapid turnover. A small pet shop may well have had its stock of budgies for several weeks. Also, baby budgies should be kept separately from adults, and there is more likely to be room for this to happen in a large pet centre. Another advantage of buying from a large pet centre is the availability of expert advice from a bird specialist.

Alternatively you could buy your budgerigar directly from a breeder. If you do, again make sure the baby birds are kept in a separate cage from the rest of the flock. It is important that your bird has not made a strong emotional attachment to other birds or he will be unhappy when they are separated.

Baby budgies are not always available. There is no set breeding season as budgies breed throughout the year. If no baby budgies are in stock, ask when the next ones are coming in; you might not have to wait very long. If they do have baby birds in stock, ask how long they have been in their cages, and then add six weeks to get a rough estimate of their age. Ideally your budgerigar should be no more than 10 weeks old.

Adult budgies are nearly always available. Although these are a few pounds cheaper than babies, they are much more difficult to tame and train. It is worth the extra expense and possible wait to get a baby.

The youngest you can buy a budgie is about six weeks. Younger than this, a budgie might still need its parents to help feed him, so a breeder would be unlikely to sell him.

Young budgies look different from adults in the following ways:

•A young budgie has large dark eyes. An adult budgie's eyes have a white surround that develops during the first year.

•The waxy skin at the base of the beak (called the cere) is pale in a young bird. In an adult it is strong blue or mauve in males and pinky brown in females. However, do not let the colour of the cere influence your judgement too much. By the age of 10 weeks the cere can have reached adult colouration and the budgie is still young enough for you to buy.

• A young budgie has a striped forehead. These stripes disappear within the first few months leaving the head a plain colour. The younger the budgie, the more numerous are the stripes.

• If the budgerigar is very young the wing and tail feathers are still short.

Budgerigars do not have external sex organs. The easiest way to distinguish a male from a female is the colour of the cere at the base of the beak. If your budgie is very young the cere will be so pale that it can be difficult to distinguish blue or mauve (male) from pinky brown (female). If you are unsure, ask for help from the person selling you the bird. This is one of the reasons why it is important to buy from an expert.

An expert will also make sure that sickly birds are rejected. The signs of sickness in a bird are: noisy breathing, creamy discharge from eyes and cere, fluffed plumage and dirty vent feathers. You should never buy a sick bird, and neither should you buy a bird that has been in contact with sick ones. Although he may look healthy he may well have been infected and could become ill.

Another thing to look for is a misshapen beak. A budgie's beak must close properly so the bird is able to de-hull seeds.

To recap	Things to avoid
Things to look for when buying a young budgie:	• Signs of adulthood – white eye surround, unstriped forehead
• Large black eyes	• Signs of illness – noisy breathing, discharge from eyes and cere, dirty
• A striped forehead	vent feathers, fluffed plumage and
• Short tail feathers	misshaped beak

Buying a budgie with the right temperament is also important. You need a bright, inquisitive bird which has not formed strong bonds with other budgerigars.

Imagine you are looking into a cage of young male budgerigars trying to decide which one to buy:

Bird One is sitting on a perch chattering loudly and confidently.
Birds Two and Three are sitting close together kissing.
Bird Four is sitting quietly apart from the others; he looks half asleep and shows no sign of shyness as you approach.
Bird Five is on the floor of the cage searching busily for dropped seeds.

Avoid Budgie One. He has already found his voice and will not be interested in learning how to talk.

Avoid Budgies Two and Three. They have bonded together. They will be unhappy if they are separated and it will be difficult to establish a relationship with either of them.

Avoid Budgie Four. He could be ill. A lack of natural shyness can be a symptom that the bird is sickening for something.

Budgie Five is the one to choose. He is full of curiosity and has not yet formed a bond with other birds.

When you buy a budgie you will be given a small box to carry him home in. The box has air holes and the budgie will be reasonably comfortable, but get him home as soon as possible and transfer him to his cage.

> **To recap**
> Your budgie should be:
> • Not too talkative
> • Inquisitive
> • Without emotional attachments to other birds

Although you must be sensible in choosing a bird you may also find that you fall for a particular budgie. This is a good basis for building a bond between you.

When I first saw Rainbow I was not really intending to buy a bird immediately. I had gone to the pet centre to see what kind of selection they had. It was 26 November 1992 – a memorable day as it turned out.

Rainbow was just seven weeks old. He was a beautiful, healthy bird of an unusual dark turquoise colour which shaded through blue and green to yellow, immediately suggesting his name. I watched his bright, intelligent eyes as he busily explored the floor of the cage and I could see that he was of the right temperament. Another budgie in the cage was bullying one of his companions and I was so worried that Rainbow might be bullied that I was determined to buy him straight away.

Although I had a cage, it was stored in the loft and needed to be washed and prepared. Even so, I bought Rainbow, took him home and kept him in his travel box for about half an hour while I hastily made all the preparations. No harm was done and I had the budgie I really wanted. So, although it may be sensible to have everything ready before you buy your bird, do not be too bound by what you read in books. There are times when it is right for your heart to rule your head.

Unfortunately, Rainbow did not keep his spectacular colouring. The dark turquoise faded to the more usual bluey-green. Although I have never for a moment regretted my impulse to buy him I would warn against being too influenced by colour in your decision to buy a young bird.Also, do not let yourself be put off by feeding and hygiene instructions which can seem rather intimidating. If your budgie is happy and has enough exercise, he will naturally stay healthy. All you need is the following simple routine:

Daily:
- Throw away uneaten seeds and replenish
- Change water container
- Brush droppings off the cage floor sandpaper

Weekly:
- Offer budgie a bath once or twice a week

- Replace sandpaper and wash and dry the bottom of the cage

Monthly:
- Clean and disinfect food dispensers, rinse and dry well
- Wash water dispensers and toys with washing-up liquid, and rinse very well
- Clean the bars of the cage

Training

The first day or two are vital in getting your relationship with your budgie off to a good start. You should buy your budgie at the start of a weekend or, even better, a long weekend or holiday, to ensure you can devote enough time to him.

All your dealings with your new budgie should be done very slowly, very gently and very quietly. He has to have time to understand what is happening and adjust to it. Even a simple thing like opening his cage door should take a long time. Do not be tempted to hurry. As long as you do not scare him, your budgie will rapidly gain confidence and, in two or three days, you will be able to move more quickly.

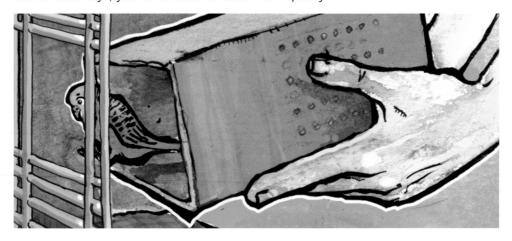

When you get your new budgie home, check that all windows and doors are closed. Then decide what method you are going to use to get him out of his travel box and into his cage. Work out beforehand exactly what you are going to do. If you have several perches in the cage it might be a good idea to remove one or more to give you enough room. Leave the perch that is in the best position for you to reach when you teach your budgie to perch on your finger. Also leave a perch that is close to the feeding containers so that the budgie can hop down and reach his food.

Practise opening and shutting the cage door without making a sound and with no sudden jerky movements. You may find you need to adjust the catch or hinges to ensure maximum smoothness.

The simplest way of transferring your bird to its cage is to put one end of the travel box into the cage close to a perch, open it slowly, and then wait until the budgie emerges. You could tilt the box slightly to encourage the budgie out, but let him take his own time. Half close the door of the cage to reduce the gap around the sides of the box. It is possible that your budgie might panic and try to escape.

An alternative method is to hold the box so that its open end is against the floor of the cage. The budgie then comes out onto the floor rather than a perch. If you do this you will have to pick the bird up gently in your hand and put it on a perch, as it will be much happier high up where it can have a good view of its surroundings.

I prefer a third method, which allows you the maximum opportunity to handle the bird.

Work over a pouffe or cushions so there will be no risk of harm if you drop the bird. Gently open the box. Look inside to see the position of the budgie, then either reach in and gently ease him out or tilt the box so that he slides into your hand. Once he is out, drop the box (it will fall silently onto the cushions) and cup the budgie in both hands. Cradle him lovingly against your breast if you like, but keep your hands absolutely still. If your hands move he may start to panic. Carry him to his cage and put him on the perch you have chosen as being the most convenient. Remember, all your movements should have been planned in advance. Remove your hands in the way that is least frightening for him and close the cage door very slowly, making sure that there is no loud click. All the time you have been doing this talk to your budgie soothingly in a soft voice or whisper. Quiet background music will also help to keep him calm.

The advantage of handling your budgie straight away is that he learns that he will come to no harm in your hands. He might not be the only one who needs this kind of reassurance; if you are a first-time owner, you will need to get used to handling your budgie.

When your budgie is safely in his cage, do not go away and leave him. Stay within sight. If you have to move around, do so very slowly and smoothly.

Make loving noises to him in a low voice. Remember that he is still a baby and treat him as such. Say his name and phrases like "Pretty boy" and "Who's gorgeous?" over and over again. He will soon get the message that you are a friend, and he will very quickly learn to recognise his name. You will be able to see your budgie relaxing as he gets used to you and his cage.

After about half an hour he should be settled enough to start his first perching lesson. It is important to start training him straight away in order to build up a close rapport. Perching lessons are best done before the bird is able to fly properly, and his wings soon become strong.

Lesson one: perching on your finger

Remove your watch, rings and bracelets and roll up your sleeve so that your arm is bare. Moving very slowly and quietly, open the cage door. From the moment you open the door your movements should be almost imperceptible.

Do not try to soothe your budgie with loving phrases while he is having a lesson as it is important that he concentrates on the task in hand. While you are teaching him to perch on your finger just say "Up, up" encouragingly. He will learn to associate the word 'up' with perching in other contexts, such as in Lesson Four when he perches on your shoulder (see page 21).

Move your finger towards the budgie extremely slowly, keeping the rest of your hand curled up as small as possible. The bird will find the finger less threatening than an entire hand. Do not point your finger at your budgie. Even the most good-natured of birds will peck at a finger he thinks is going to poke him. Bend your finger so that he can step onto the middle knuckle.

Keep going steadily but stop the moment your budgie becomes apprehensive and wait until he relaxes. If necessary, withdraw your finger slightly and then start to move it towards him again. Your budgie will respond in one of two ways: either he will accept your approach or he will panic. If the bird starts to panic withdraw your finger completely (still moving slowly), close the cage door and stay close to the cage. Make loving noises and wait until your budgie relaxes before trying again. Do not give up or feel a failure; remember that you and your bird can only get better.

Persist gently but firmly and eventually your finger will be in position parallel to his chest. Still moving extremely slowly, stroke your budgie under the curve of his chest and say "Up, up" to encourage him to lift one foot and grasp your finger. Do not make the mistake of stroking your budgie's legs or you might knock him off his perch – a disaster at this stage of training!

Concentrate on what you want your budgie to do and do not be nervous: he will not bite you. He will soon lift one of his feet and hold onto your finger. This can be a critical moment for you both; if you are not used to handling a budgie the feel of his scaly claw pressed against your skin can be disconcerting. Do not change your mind or show any fear or the budgie will sense it and start to panic.

Continue to push against his chest and say "Up, up" to encourage him to lift his

other foot and perch on your finger properly. This will not be easy as your budgie will be determined to keep hold of the perch. If he shows any signs of fear stay still with one of his feet grasping your finger. Be determined, you are nearly there – one little step should do it.

Eventually your budgie will let go of his perch and grasp your finger with both feet. Wait until he has a steady grip, then slowly move your finger away from the perch. Keep still while your budgie gets used to being on your finger, then carry him round the perch to the other side. Be very careful not to knock against the side of the cage or to bump the bird itself while you are doing this. Any sudden sound or jerky movement will frighten him.

You may find you have to hold your hand in an awkward position in order to make the journey as smooth as possible while keeping your other fingers curled up tightly. Persevere and do not be tempted to rush. Once round to the other side, press the base of the budgie's chest gently against the perch and say "Up, up". He will step up onto the perch. Now remove your hand carefully.

Wait for a few moments, then repeat the lesson once more. When he has perched on your finger twice, slowly remove your hand from the cage and close the door gently. Stay beside the cage murmuring endearments to your budgie.

Your budgie will need many rest breaks during the day for sleeping and feeding. It may take him an hour or two to hop down from his perch and discover his food. In the meantime he will start to feel hungry. After he has had Lesson One and before he finds his food is a good time to make a first approach with your hand.

Hold your hand palm up with your thumb curled tightly and your fingers close together so that it looks as small as possible. Put a pile of seeds on your fingers, including small bits of millet spray which are a budgie's favourite. Approach the budgie with your hand and offer him the seeds, moving very slowly and quietly. Be ready to retreat if he shows signs of panic but persevere until he is able to feed from your hand. If he does not show any interest withdraw and try again a little later.

It is not necessary for him to perch on your hand yet. At this stage you just want him to get used to it and be aware that it will do him no harm. Do not be too impatient for your budgie to make progress on the first day. Part of what you are achieving is to get to know each other and build up trust.

Although you should always close windows and doors before you open the cage door your budgie is unlikely to make a bid to escape from the cage. If he does flutter from the cage do not worry; he will not be able to fly properly yet and he will quickly come to rest somewhere in the room. Let him exercise his wings for a while as this will strengthen them and is a natural process in learning how to fly.

When you are ready to put him back in his cage, carefully pick him up with both hands and cradle him against your chest to avoid damaging him. Move very slowly and keep your hands still once you are holding him. Carry him back to his cage, place him on his perch and slowly remove your hands. Although it does no harm for him to escape from his cage, do not encourage him to fly yet. It is much easier to teach him to perch before he flies.

Your budgie is more likely to try to escape from your attentions by jumping off his perch onto the floor of the cage. Do not let him get away with this as it will become a habit every time you approach him with your finger. Give him a moment to calm down, then pick him up, put him back on the perch and remove your hand very slowly. Do not repeat the lesson immediately but stay near the cage murmuring endearments before trying again. If you move slowly enough your budgie should remain relaxed and not try to avoid you.

Lesson two: perching on the hand

When your budgie is happy to perch on your finger, start training him to perch on your hand. This will probably be on the second or third day.

Choose your moment carefully. Do not interrupt the bird if he is eating or sleeping.

Treat him with respect; in particular, you should respect his fear.

You will already have fed your budgie from your hand. This may have helped him be less fearful of it, but do not be too sure; be as slow and careful in your approach as you were with your finger. It will not be long before you can start speeding up. Put seeds on your hand. Curl up your thumb, hold your fingers as flat as possible and open the cage door very slowly and quietly. If your budgie seems agitated, close the door and wait for a few minutes before trying again. Whenever the cage door is shut you can murmur endearments to calm your budgie down. Once the lesson starts, only use the appropriate phrase. When you have managed to reach the bird with your hand without frightening him, stroke him under his chest and say "Up, up". When he is standing on your hand move him slowly away from the perch and wait for a few moments. He should continue to feed on the seed you are holding. Slowly move your hand round the perch to the other side and encourage your budgie to step up onto the perch. There will be little room to manoeuvre but you must keep your hand in the same position no matter how uncomfortable it is. Your budgie will take fright if your fingers move.

Lesson three: perching on the cage

Lesson Three should be attempted around day three when your budgie is confident to perch on your finger. This time, instead of moving him round to the other side of the perch bring him out of the cage and encourage him to perch in the doorway. When your budgie is clinging to the doorway, slowly remove your hand. Give him an opportunity to look around and understand where he is; then say "Up, up" and make him perch on your hand once more. Return him to his perch, slowly remove your hand and praise him softly but effusively. Repeat the lesson, give your budgie a 15-minute break, and then try once more. This time you can encourage your budgie to perch on top of his cage. The more often you perch him on the cage the more confident your budgie will become. He will also learn to recognise the cage and be able to return to it when he is allowed to fly freely in the room. Although these lessons are labelled one, two and three, do not expect steady progress in these early days. You may find that for no apparent reason your budgie seems to forget everything he has learnt. If this happens do not give up; start again with patience and persistence and you are bound to be successful in the end. Repeat the first three lessons until you and your budgerigar are comfortable with one another. At this stage let other people have the budgie on their fingers. Make sure they understand that they must hold their finger absolutely still. Manoeuvre the budgie into the correct position for him to step up onto it then stay close so that you can take him back to his cage if he becomes uneasy.

Lesson four: perching on your shoulder

Tie your hair back and remove any jewellery such as dangling earrings that might frighten your budgie. Put some millet on your shoulder, just the seeds, not a spray. Slowly open your budgie's cage, get him to perch on your finger and remove him from the cage. Encourage your budgie to perch on your shoulder by holding him so that he can step up easily. The first time you do this he will wonder what is going on and may feel apprehensive at being so close to your face. If he seems too frightened move him away from your shoulder and wait for him to relax before slowly moving him close again. Say "Up" in a soft voice. He will quickly recognise the word and know what to do. Do not move when he is on your shoulder and keep your head very still. He may or may not eat the millet seeds. If he does, wait until he finishes eating and then get him to perch on your finger again.

Move him away from you, pause for a few moments, then slowly move him back to your shoulder, encouraging him to perch once more. When he has perched twice, take him back onto your finger and carry him back to the cage. Praise him.

Later on, when he is used to being on your shoulder, your budgie will want to show his affection by nibbling your ear and cheek as if he was kissing you. Do not let him nibble your mouth as this is unhygienic.

After your budgie is happy to perch on your shoulder you can train him to perch on your head. Do this in front of a mirror so you can see that you are holding him in the right position.

Using the same method, teach your budgie to perch in different places in the room. You should fix up one or two perches for him away from his cage. Put these high but not so high that you cannot reach him easily. Let him examine the perch from your finger while you say "What's that?" in an interested voice. Hold a spray of millet on the other side of the perch so the budgie has to lean across to eat it. Move the millet away so the budgie has to stand on the perch to eat it. Let him stand on the perch for a while, take him off on your finger and then return him to the perch. Before he flies from the perch on his own accord take him back on your finger again and carry him to his cage.

Next time you take him to the perch, carry him there from his cage. He will soon learn to fly from his cage to the perch.

Although eventually he will like a perch high in the centre of the room he will be reluctant to go to it at first because he will feel too exposed. It will be easier to train him to go to a corner perch, especially if it is near a mirror. Teach him also to perch on the back of the sofa and arm chairs and any other place where you are happy for him to be. Do not encourage him onto the curtain rail; it might be difficult for you to reach him there.

You will probably want your budgie to play with his toys on the floor where he will have plenty of room. A small container of food or a pile of seeds on the carpet will encourage him. Kneel down slowly with the bird on your finger and hold him close to the food. He may take his time but eventually he will hop down onto the carpet to feed. He will be especially keen to go to the floor if you remove the food from his cage while you are training him.

Train him down to the floor early or he will tend to stay high. Although you must be careful not to step on him, it is worth taking the effort to train him to the floor as it is charming to watch him playing with his toys on the carpet.

After each exercise take your budgie back to his cage where he can relax and feed. Remember he is still a baby and needs lots of rest.

Lesson five: ladders

When your budgie is happy to perch on your index finger, bring him out of the cage and stroke the curve of his chest with your other index finger so he climbs up onto it. Use the key word "Up". Repeat so the budgie climbs up your index fingers as if he were climbing a ladder. Gradually move your fingers further apart so he has to hop up.

Once he has learnt to hop on to your finger you will not have to stroke his chest to get him off his perch, just hold your finger close.

> **To recap**
> - Lesson One: Encourage your budgie to perch on your finger and transport him within his cage
> - Lesson Two: Encourage your budgie to perch on your hand and transport him within the cage
> - Lesson Three: Transport your budgie in and out of the cage and encourage him to perch in the doorway and on the bars
> - Lesson Four: Teach your budgie to perch on your shoulder, head and different places in the room including the floor
> - Lesson Five: Teach your budgie to jump up from finger to finger

Further training

You may want to teach your budgie more than the five basic lessons I have described. For example, I always wanted to be able to click my fingers and have my bird fly to my hand so I taught Rainbow to do this.

I removed him from the cage on my finger and put him on one of his other perches – a circular perch which hung high in an archway. I then put a small amount of food on the back of my hand, held it close to the perch and let him start to eat the seeds. I slowly moved my hand away and said "Come, Rainbow, come." I held the seeds just out of his reach and, after some hesitation, he stepped onto my hand and continued to eat.

Once he had got used to doing that I held my hand a little further away from the perch so he had to jump further across. Every time I wanted him to come I said "Come, Rainbow, come" so that eventually he would understand what he had to do when he heard the phrase.

Once Rainbow was steady on my hand I slowly straightened my arm so that he was held well away from my body. It sounds easy written down but this was the first lesson that I gave up in despair. After three days of effort my arm ached with holding it out while Rainbow stared at me suspiciously from his perch. I decided it was not worth the effort and did not bother with it for a few days. Then one evening I was sitting on the sofa and Rainbow was twittering happily on top of his cage. Not expecting any response I held out my arm and said "Come, Rainbow, come." I was about to put my arm down again when he flew from the cage straight to my hand – and was most disconcerted to find no seeds were there! You can imagine how delighted I was.

I recommend anyone who is getting fed up with a lesson to leave it for a couple of days. You may be in for a surprise when you go back to it.

You will find that once you have established a relationship of love and trust with your budgie you will be able to teach him many things. You must take lessons slowly. Remember that budgies will always be frightened of new things; it is nature's way of helping them to survive. Even now, Rainbow is frightened by a new toy and has to be encouraged to play with it.

A budgie needs to feed often, so use food to attract him. This is even more effective if you remove the food from his cage so that he gets hungry. Make what is expected of him as clear as possible. Use voice as well as gesture in your command and praise him gently and effusively when he responds correctly. A budgie thrives on attention and, once he has lost his fear of you, your budgie will enjoy his lessons.

> **To recap**
> • Move very slowly and smoothly every time you do something new
> • Use food to attract your budgie
> • Use a single phrase during the lesson
> • Praise him afterwards

By now your budgie will be tame enough for you to start to teach him to talk. How long it takes to get to this stage depends on how much time you have been able to spend with your budgie. I started teaching Rainbow to talk after I had had him for just three weeks. This swift rate of progress was achieved by devoting the first two days to taming him and all my spare time in subsequent weeks – after family, household chores and a part-time job had taken their toll. I even wore the same top for many days so that Rainbow could recognise me easily. It was worth all the effort. If you lay good foundations you can made swift progress.

Teach your budgie to talk

When your budgie is perched on your finger, hold him about 25 cm (10in) away from your face, look at him and start to speak. If he is in a listening mood, he will sit still on your finger with his head cocked forward.

Choose a simple, short phrase to start with and say it to your budgie, slowly and precisely. Articulate well, moving your lips more than usual to emphasise the words.

At first your budgie will not understand what is happening and may want to fly away. If you see him preparing to fly, stop talking and distract him by putting him on a perch or giving him something to eat. You can try again later when he may be more receptive.

Talk very slowly during the first few sessions. Start by saying the phrase just two or three times, gradually building up the number of times you repeat it. As the budgie starts to learn the phrase you can increase almost to the speed of normal speech and repeat the phrase at least 30 times. Always speak very clearly and keep exactly the same intonation.

The more often you say the phrase the quicker your budgie will learn it. If you are able to repeat a phrase 30 times for five or more sessions a day your budgie should be

able to learn it in about two weeks. You will hear him repeating key words to himself as he rehearses the phrase but do not be tempted to teach him the words individually. Emphasise the words he is finding difficult by saying them very clearly and perhaps more than once but only teach them as part of the phrase. Wait until he is able to repeat the phrase perfectly before teaching him something new.

Once a budgie has learnt a phrase he will not forget it, but you should go through his whole repertoire regularly or gradually he will use some phrases less. Your budgie will enjoy this, as he recognises the sounds you are making. If I pause when I am going through Rainbow's phrases, he chirrups encouragingly as if urging me to continue.

When choosing a new phrase for your budgie to learn, decide upon something with a good rhythm and easy words. An easy word for a budgie is one with plenty of vowels and not too many consonants.

WHO'S A LOVELY BOY!!

It is a good idea to teach your budgie to say his address so that if he gets lost he can be returned. Poor Rainbow had to learn to say the name of our town, which is not at all an easy word for a budgie. However, I started him on much easier phrases. After he had been with us for seven weeks he was saying, "Alan is a cheeky boy." This delighted my nine-year-old son (Alan) and formed the basis of a firm friendship between boy and bird.

Rainbow's second phrase was based on my husband's name (Derek) and learnt just two weeks later: "Derek, shut up!"

I have had great fun choosing phrases for Rainbow to say. The joke has worn rather thin on some I thought amusing at the time, for example, "Is Cilla black or white?" Some have proved unexpectedly difficult for Rainbow to say. "Have a break, have a Kit Kat" is very rarely completed, as Rainbow usually stops after "Kit". On the whole, the phrases that work best are those which Rainbow might say if we were having a conversation.

You will be able to teach your bird new phrases throughout his life but you must run through his old phrases with him daily or he will say them less often. As long as he has heard you speaking he will spend happy hours talking to himself, perfecting the phrases he has heard you saying. Also, when he hears music, he will talk.

By teaching your budgie to talk you ensure that he gets lots of attention, not only from you but also from admiring friends and relations. Communicating with each other in this way builds a strong bond between you and your pet and ensures you get the best out of your budgie. A tape can be used to reinforce his memory once he knows the phrases but it is not an alternative to communicating with the bird personally. As the

> **To recap**
> - Choose a rhythmic phrase with easy words
> - Hold the budgie on your finger 25 cm (10) inches from your face
> - Repeat the phrase very slowly and precisely a few times at first and then with increasing speed up to 30 times
> - Have about five teaching sessions a day

number of phrases increases you might have difficulty remembering them all, so you should write them down.

Teaching your bird to speak will not stop it communicating in its own way and you should be alert to what it is trying to say. A screech means your bird is upset about something. Try to find out what it is. Perhaps a sudden noise has upset him, or the television is too loud, or birds flying past the window have frightened him. I find that the thing that most upsets Rainbow is when the light is too bright. Do something about it if you can; do not leave your budgie screeching.

> **Rainbow's phrases:**
> - Who's a cheeky boy then?
> - Alan is a cheeky boy.
> - Derek, shut up!
> - I'm an Arsenal fan.
> - Is Cilla black or white?
> - I'm not stupid, I can speak.
> - Alan is my best friend.
> - Please no smoking, no farting, thank you.
> - I live at .. (address).
> - Je m'appelle Rainbow.
> - Je peux parler français bien que je suis anglais.
> - Please what's the time, I'm starving.
> - Guten Tag, Flip. Wie geht's.
> - I'm a clever bird, aren't I? I can speak German too.
> - Have a break, have a Kit Kat.
> - Would you like a coffee?
> - I'm a good boy, yes? I'm a good boy.
> - Please be quiet and let me speak.
> - Don't ask me why – I hate cats.
> - I t'ought I taw a puddy tatt.
> - What's the matter?
> - Do you want a kiss? (followed by the sound of a kiss)
> - Come, Rainbow, come.
> - Do you want some sweeties? Go on, then.

Daily care

Freedom is a good thing for a bird but it is important that you tame your bird before you allow him to live freely in your house. A few basic precautions should be taken to prepare your living room for a free-living budgie.

Put a fire guard in front of an open fire. Naked flames, including candles, are dangerous for a budgerigar. Patio doors and picture windows should have net curtains or strips of tape over them so that the budgie does not fly into them.

If you have trained your budgie to use perches he will spend most of his time on them and on top of his cage. You can protect the floor underneath from droppings if you like but it is not really necessary. Budgie droppings are small and odourless. They should not stain carpets or glazed cottons and other furnishing fabrics. They dry rapidly and can be vacuumed or brushed up easily.

Branches, whether real or artificial, have an advantage over perches, being of variable diameters so that the budgie exercises his feet when he perches on them. Real branches (from deciduous trees and shrubs) have to be cleaned thoroughly to be free from wild bird droppings. Plastic branches can be bought from pet shops and are designed to fit into a cage. Rainbow loves to sit on a display of artificial blossoms on our window-sill so that he can look out at the front garden. Even though they are now his favourite I had to train him to perch on them at first.

Keep your living room reasonably clean. Dust can give your budgie respiratory infections and sharp grit can cause problems if he swallows it. A budgie will naturally search for grit in your carpet or potted plants. Since birds have no teeth a budgie needs to swallow grit and keep it in his crop to help grind up seeds for digestion. You can buy suitable grit, but this will not stop your budgie scavenging for more, so use your vacuum cleaner regularly.

Avoid draughts. Although budgies are fairly tolerant of changes in temperature they are very susceptible to draughts and can catch a deadly chill. Make sure that cupboards and equipment such as stereos are flat against the wall, or as close as possible, so that your budgie cannot get stuck behind them.

To recap
Preparing the living room:
- Guard fire
- Protect picture windows and patio doors
- Keep room clean
- Avoid draughts
- Do not leave large gaps behind furniture

It is possible to buy a bath that attaches onto the side of a cage but it is much more convenient to allow a tame budgie to have his bath on the floor of your living room. Any container will do as long as it holds about an inch of water. A mirror or toy placed in the bath may entice your budgie into the water if he is reluctant to take the plunge.

Rainbow is very fussy about bathing. He inspects the water carefully and will not go in if there is a speck of dirt. This is a good instinct as bathing in contaminated water is dangerous for a budgie. He also refuses to go in if I try to warm the water up. He prefers it cold, straight from the tap in the summer, although I do take the chill off it in winter.

I wish Rainbow was more enthusiastic about bathing. It is charming to watch a budgie splashing happily in his bath. It is also essential to the bird's health as it keeps the feathers clean.

Encourage your budgie to bathe at least once a week; more if he enjoys it. Mornings are the best time as the bird must be completely dry when it retires for the night.

There is plenty of room on the living room floor for all Rainbow's toys. Among his favourites are a weighted ball with a mirror attached to it that rights itself when he pecks it over, a bell which he can throw and a ladder seesaw. Inside the cage he has a tassel with a bell which he also loves. These toys are all specially designed for budgies but he also gets a lot of pleasure from any little things he can play with, from old baby toys to kitchen bits and pieces.

Budgies have a sense of humour. One of Rainbow's favourite jokes is to push the remote control off the sofa or coffee table so that I have to pick it up.

When we first tamed Rainbow we let him out of his cage regularly for short periods of time. I always stayed with him to make sure he came to no harm. The period of his freedom increased until now I let Rainbow out of his cage first thing in the morning and he usually goes to his cage himself during the day and for his night's sleep. If the lights and TV disturb him, we cover his cage with a cloth or take it to another room.

Although the living room is Rainbow's main territory he has become more courageous as he has matured and is happy to come to me when I call him from other parts of the house. We now have to close the living room door when we are out in case he goes exploring on his own and gets into trouble.

Living with any pet needs some adjustments and the amount of time and effort you spend when the pet is young pays dividends in later life. A budgie can live more than 20 years. He is cheap to feed, is easy to leave with friends when you go on holiday and full of fun and affection – a wonderful, intelligent little companion.

When you are training your budgie you may imagine that you are making no progress but do not give up. If you are patient and persevere you will succeed and the rewards will be great for both of you.

Index